ISBN:979-8-9990779-2-9

This book is intended as a practical resource and
informational guide. It is not a substitute for professional
counseling or therapy. The author and publisher assume
no liability for outcomes related to the use of this book.

YOU ARE NOT TOO MUCH

The Inner Work of Becoming Fully Seen

by

Ethan Starke

"You Were Never Too Much—They Were Too Little With You"

Let me begin with a truth most of us are too tired to pretend away:

You were never too much.

Not your feelings.
Not your intensity.
Not your silence that held more truth than someone else's whole performance.

You were never too much.
They just didn't know what to do with all of you.
So they called your longing excessive.
Your honesty dramatic.
Your neediness a flaw.

But here's the thing:
Too much is what the world becomes when it's been starving for real for too long.

This is not a dating book.
It's not a 5-step program to make someone fall in love with you.
It's not even about how to be chosen.
This is about *choosing yourself in full view.*

This book is for the ones who have carried their hearts like fire:
Lighting the way. Burning silently.
Always at risk of being misunderstood, or worse—extinguished.

It's for the overthinkers, the deep feelers, the ones who've kept a little less of themselves each time just to stay in the room.
This is your invitation to take up space.
Messy, magical, *real* space.

We were not made for performance.
We were made for presence.

What follows isn't advice.
It's a reckoning.
It's a mirror.
It's a permission slip.
And maybe, by the end, it's a homecoming.

You are not too much.
You are just finally enough—for yourself.

Where Did You Start Dimming?

The Early Lessons

Somewhere along the way, many of us learned that shrinking
made things easier.
Not because anyone said it directly—few lessons this deep ever
are—but because smallness seemed to smooth the edges off
living.

It wasn't one single moment that taught this.
It was a series of quiet adjustments.
Moments when excitement was met with a sidelong glance.
Times when curiosity felt too big for the room.
The quiet recalibrations made when needing something—
comfort, clarity, understanding—seemed like asking too much.

At first, these lessons feel almost invisible.
They settle in the body before they reach the mind.
A slight hesitation before speaking.
A careful check on how much joy to show.
A quiet inventory of what's safe to share and what isn't.

Shrinking doesn't announce itself.
It moves in slowly, wrapping itself around the parts of the self that
once stretched easily into the world.
And over time, what felt like learning how to survive begins to
look more like learning how to disappear.

Few people call it disappearing.
It's usually framed as maturity.
Learning how to be agreeable.
Learning how not to make things harder for anyone else.
Learning how to be a person who doesn't take up more than their share.

But under the surface, a different kind of learning takes root.
Learning how to withhold parts of the self that once felt ordinary.
Learning how to apologize without speaking.
Learning how to live smaller, not because smaller feels right—but because smaller feels safer.

The Weight of Disappearance

The trouble with shrinking is that it rarely stays small.
What begins as a few careful edits can become the way a person
moves through the world.
Not bold, not broken—just distant. Present but not fully here.

At first, it might look like success.
The ability to stay quiet in a meeting when others rush to speak.
The knack for making others comfortable, even when it costs
something invisible.
The patience to listen without needing to be heard in return.

From the outside, it's easy to mistake this for strength.
Patience. Resilience. Maturity.

But on the inside, the cost accumulates.
The distance grows.
Not just from others—but from the self.

The body remembers what the mind tries to forget.
The tightening of the chest before sharing an opinion.
The pause before admitting a need.
The way the heart folds itself a little smaller with every unspoken
truth.

Over time, something harder to name begins to settle in:
A heaviness that rest can't lift.
A dull ache under the skin of daily life.
A sense that somewhere along the way, something essential was
misplaced.

Not lost all at once, but in pieces.
A part of the voice left behind in that meeting.
A part of the laughter softened until it sounded acceptable.
A part of the heart kept quiet until it forgot how to speak.

This is not the dramatic kind of loss that draws attention.
It's the quieter kind.
The kind that leaves a person looking perfectly fine to everyone else.
The kind that leaves them wondering why fine never feels like enough.

Shrinking is praised because it looks like cooperation.
It's rewarded because it keeps things easy.

But what no one says is how heavy it is to live a life that fits someone else's comfort better than it fits the shape of the soul.

Where Safety Becomes Distance

Safety, at first, feels like a victory.
The safety of being accepted.
The safety of avoiding conflict.
The safety of knowing which parts of the self are welcome and which are not.

But safety bought through shrinking leaves behind a residue—an invisible distance.

Not the distance of solitude, which can be nourishing, but the distance of absence.
A kind of quiet unrooting from the self.

It can be difficult to name at first.
There's no single moment when it becomes clear.
Just small realizations:
A conversation ends and it feels like no one was really there.
A moment of laughter, and yet something inside remains untouched.
A gathering of friends, and still the sense of being unseen, even in the middle of it.

The distance isn't only from others.
It's from the parts of the self left behind for the sake of peace.
The opinions unspoken.
The longings silenced.
The instincts second-guessed.

Over time, this distance grows comfortable, like clothing worn so often it feels like skin.
It can even masquerade as independence:
A life where nothing is needed from anyone.
A life that claims not to mind being misunderstood.

But beneath that posture, there is a different kind of loneliness.
Not the loneliness of being alone, but the loneliness of not being known.

It is one thing to be unseen by others.
It is another to become unseen by the self.

The Quiet Cost of Adaptation

Adaptation can look like resilience.
It can feel like strength.
The ability to move through spaces without asking for too much.
The ability to weather conversations without needing to be fully understood.
The ability to live with parts of the self carefully placed out of sight.

At first, it may even feel like wisdom:
knowing when to stay silent, knowing when to lower the volume of a feeling, knowing when to step back rather than forward.

But adaptation, when it demands the erasure of the self, carries a cost that is often not seen until it has been paid.

It begins with the small things:
The joy tempered so it doesn't overwhelm.
The excitement edited until it seems reasonable.
The sadness kept private so it doesn't become inconvenient.

It spreads slowly:
The way desires become quiet suggestions rather than clear expressions.
The way ambitions become private dreams, rarely spoken aloud.
The way love becomes cautious, careful, measured—less a reaching out and more a holding back.

Adaptation teaches how to survive a world that doesn't always welcome the full weight of a person's being.
But survival is not the same as living.

Living demands a different kind of courage—the courage to stay whole even when wholeness is misunderstood.
The courage to show up without editing.
The courage to want, to ask, to reveal.

For many, there comes a moment—quiet, almost unremarkable —when the cost becomes clear.
A realization that the safety won was never free.
A recognition that the belonging earned through shrinking is not the kind of belonging that can sustain a life.

It is a difficult truth:
The adaptations that once protected can become the very things that imprison.
The strategies that once kept the world manageable can become the reasons the world feels so distant.

And yet, this realization is not an end.
It is a beginning.
A beginning marked not by the need to become someone new, but by the invitation to return to what was never truly lost.

To begin the work of unshrinking.
To allow the full shape of the self to take up space again.
To risk being seen, not as someone improved, but as someone *real*.

The Myth of Being "Too Much"

Where the Myth Begins

For many, the idea of being "too much" doesn't start with a single accusation.
It builds slowly, gathered from glances, silences, and the careful ways people turn away.

It can begin in places that are supposed to be safe:
Family tables where big feelings are unwelcome.
Classrooms where curiosity is seen as disruption.
Friendships where honesty is praised until it becomes uncomfortable.

Over time, the lesson becomes less about what is allowed and more about what is expected.
Stay small.
Stay manageable.
Stay easy to handle.

The myth of being "too much" often finds its power not in cruelty, but in the quiet conditioning that asks for less without ever saying it outright.
Less feeling.
Less need.
Less truth.

It becomes easy to internalize this expectation.
To start believing that emotions are liabilities.
That needs are burdens.
That wanting to be seen fully is selfish or naive.

And because belonging matters—because connection is necessary—many learn to comply.
They shrink the parts of themselves that feel risky.
They moderate their enthusiasm.
They dilute their grief.
They make their joy quieter, their anger softer, their love less demanding.

The myth works best when it goes unchallenged.
When it seeps into the background of a life, shaping choices, relationships, even the way a person sees themselves.

It teaches that being fully alive is dangerous.
That wholeness must be traded for acceptance.
That too muchness is something to be managed, apologized for, or hidden away.

But the real danger is not in feeling too deeply or wanting too much.
The real danger is in living a life edited to fit someone else's comfort.

How the Myth Shapes Us

Once the idea takes hold—that certain parts of the self are excessive, inconvenient, or embarrassing—it starts to shape everything.

It shapes the way emotions are carried.
Not as signals to be trusted, but as problems to be hidden.

Grief becomes something to manage in private.
Anger becomes something to mute into irritation.
Joy becomes something to ration in case it draws too much attention.

It shapes the way relationships are built.
Choosing partners, friends, and communities not by who sees the whole self, but by who seems willing to tolerate a reduced version.
Adapting conversations to avoid discomfort.
Keeping certain dreams and opinions locked away, not out of secrecy, but out of learned caution.

It shapes the way risks are taken.
Hesitating to speak a truth that feels too raw.
Second-guessing instincts that feel too strong.
Avoiding opportunities that might demand too much visibility, too much vulnerability.

And in the background, it shapes the way worth is measured.
Not by wholeness, but by acceptability.
Not by being alive, but by being agreeable.

For many, this shaping becomes invisible after a while.
It feels like common sense.
It feels like wisdom.

Stay agreeable.
Stay reasonable.
Stay manageable.

But there's a cost:
A life lived within limits that were never chosen.
A self trimmed down to fit spaces that were never built to hold it.

The myth doesn't just limit the size of feelings.
It limits the size of a life.

The Cost of Believing the Myth

Believing the myth of being "too much" doesn't happen all at once.
It happens gradually, until it becomes difficult to separate personal truth from the learned habit of self-erasure.

The cost is subtle at first.
Opportunities passed over.
Conversations left unfinished.
Parts of the self set aside for the sake of being easier to love, easier to understand, easier to manage.

But over time, the cost compounds.

Dreams start to feel unrealistic—not because they are impossible, but because they demand a fullness that has been taught to feel dangerous.
Desires become smaller, more practical, more acceptable—not because they lose their urgency, but because reaching for them risks being misunderstood.

Relationships, too, are affected.
Connections built on half-truths create an ache that is difficult to name: the loneliness of being surrounded but unseen.
The safety of being accepted becomes hollow when it comes at the expense of being known.

Even solitude, once a refuge, can lose its comfort when the self being kept company is only a fraction of the whole.

The deeper cost is harder to measure:
A loss of trust—not just in others, but in the self.
A quiet belief that instincts are wrong, feelings are liabilities,
wants are selfish.
A life lived not fully claimed, but carefully managed.

The myth persuades many to believe that if they can just be less,
they will be enough.
Less needy.
Less emotional.
Less complicated.

But lessness is not wholeness.
And a life built on managing perception will always feel hollow at
its center.

Dismantling the Myth

The myth of being "too much" survives because it remains unchallenged.
It feeds on silence.
It grows in the spaces where discomfort is met with withdrawal instead of curiosity.

Dismantling it begins quietly—not with grand declarations, but with small, persistent acts of return.

It begins with noticing:
Noticing when a feeling rises and the instinct is to push it away.
Noticing when a truth presses forward and the impulse is to soften it for the sake of ease.
Noticing when a desire surfaces and shame arrives before permission.

Noticing is not judgment.
It's a form of remembering.

The myth thrives in forgetting:
Forgetting that needs are not burdens.
Forgetting that feelings are not flaws.
Forgetting that the full expression of a life is not an inconvenience, but a right.

Dismantling the myth means learning how to stay present with the parts of the self that once seemed too large to hold.

It means asking harder questions:
Who benefits when wholeness is called selfish?

Who benefits when truth is called trouble?
Who benefits when a life is lived quietly, cautiously, halfway?

And more importantly:
What becomes possible when the full self is no longer
negotiable?

The myth unravels slowly.
It unravels when feelings are honored rather than edited.
When needs are spoken rather than hidden.
When space is taken without apology.

There is no single moment of arrival.
There is only the gradual reclaiming of ground that was quietly
surrendered.
There is only the slow, steady return to a self that was never truly
too much—only waiting for permission to be seen whole.

Love as Performance, Attachment as Survival

When Love Becomes a Performance

For many, love begins with a subtle kind of performance.
Not because there is a desire to deceive, but because early love
is often entangled with early survival.

The first lessons about love are not taught with words.
They are learned through attention withheld or given, approval
offered or withdrawn.
They are learned in the spaces where affection feels conditional:
given when certain behaviors are displayed,
withdrawn when others surface.

It doesn't take long for a pattern to emerge:
Love seems more available when certain parts of the self are
emphasized.
Compliance.
Achievement.
Pleasantness.
Containment.

And less available when other parts show up.
Anger.
Need.
Complexity.
Vulnerability.

Without being told directly, many learn that love can be earned, but only by presenting a version of the self that others find acceptable.

The performance begins early.
Learning how to anticipate what will be welcomed and what will not.
Learning how to shift posture, language, expression—not dramatically, but enough to feel safer, enough to stay close.

This isn't manipulation.
It's adaptation.
It's the quiet, often unconscious calculation made to protect the most necessary connection of all—the connection to others.

The body learns before the mind can name it:
There is a version of the self that draws people closer.
There is a version of the self that risks being left behind.

Love, once understood in this way, ceases to feel unconditional.
It becomes something to be managed.
Protected.
Maintained through vigilance and effort.

A private performance, so practiced it feels natural.
A performance not to impress, but to remain.

Attachment and the Fear of Being Left

Attachment is not a choice made in the logical mind.
It is older than language, deeper than reason.
It forms not just around people, but around patterns:
The way comfort is offered,
the way distance is created,
the way presence can feel just as fragile as absence.

When early connections teach that love can be withdrawn, the
attachment that follows carries a kind of vigilance.
It is an attachment shaped by the fear of being left,
by the belief that belonging must be maintained,
by the unspoken understanding that safety is conditional.

This fear doesn't announce itself loudly.
It shows up quietly, in small hesitations and calculations:
the instinct to say the right thing rather than the real thing,
the tendency to soften needs into suggestions,
the habit of shrinking moments of discomfort to keep others
close.

Many learn to read the emotional weather of a room before
speaking.
To anticipate shifts before they happen.
To adjust tone, volume, opinion—not to manipulate, but to
survive.

Over time, these adjustments become second nature.
Not because of weakness, but because of an early truth
absorbed in the body:
connection is essential, and loss is dangerous.

Attachment shaped by fear rarely feels like fear.
It feels like over-responsibility for the moods of others.
It feels like anxiety disguised as care.
It feels like self-erasure performed in the name of keeping peace.

At its core, it's an attempt to hold love steady.
To prevent departure by becoming whatever is safest to stay close to.
To mistake predictability for intimacy.

But this kind of attachment costs more than it gives.
It trades authenticity for security.
It trades being known for being needed.
It trades the whole self for a closeness that never fully satisfies.

When Survival Becomes Habit

What begins as a way to stay connected can harden into habit.
Adaptation becomes reflex.
Performance becomes identity.

Over time, the survival strategies used to protect connection stop
feeling like strategies at all.
They feel like personality traits.
Easygoing.
Low-maintenance.
Independent.

Underneath these labels, though, is often something quieter:
a lifetime of studying what others want before offering anything of
the self.
a lifetime of translating real needs into something smaller, safer,
more acceptable.

When survival becomes habit, the body moves ahead of the
mind.
Smiling when hurt.
Nodding when disagreeing.
Offering reassurance before asking for it in return.

Not because of manipulation, but because long ago it became
necessary.
To survive meant being attentive, agreeable, careful.
To survive meant being less visible, less complicated, less
demanding.

And when a way of surviving becomes a way of living, it becomes harder to tell the difference between what is real and what is rehearsed.
Harder to trust that connection could be possible without the performance.
Harder to believe that love could stay even when all the masks are set down.

There comes a point where the strategies that once protected become the very structures that isolate.
The life carefully built to avoid rejection becomes a life where true intimacy can't find a way in.
The relationships maintained through careful management become relationships where being fully seen feels impossible.

Habit creates safety, but it also creates distance.
Habit prevents loss, but it also prevents presence.
Habit guards against pain, but it also guards against joy.

The cost of living through habit is not immediately visible.
It shows up slowly:
in the ache of feeling unseen even in partnership,
in the exhaustion of being loved for a version of the self that never quite feels true,
in the quiet fear that being fully known would mean being fully abandoned.

Survival once required these habits.
But living—truly living—requires something different.

The Risk of Being Fully Seen

The idea of being fully seen carries its own kind of fear.
Not the fear of surface rejection, but something deeper:
the fear that if the masks are dropped, if the carefulness is set
aside, there will be nothing left to hold others near.

The risk of being seen is not just about exposure.
It is about the possibility that realness will be met not with
acceptance, but with absence.

And yet, the risk is necessary.
Because connection built on performance will never satisfy the
hunger it tries to fill.
Because belonging earned through self-erasure will never quiet
the deeper ache to be known.

Being fully seen asks for a different kind of courage.
The courage to allow emotions to surface without moderation.
The courage to voice needs without apology.
The courage to bring the whole self into the room, even when
there is no guarantee it will be welcomed.

There is no promise of safety in this risk.
No assurance that all will go well.

Some connections will shift under the weight of realness.
Some relationships will falter when the performance ends.
Some spaces will prove too small to hold what is true.

But the risk is not about guaranteeing a result.
It is about reclaiming the self that was never meant to be
negotiated away.

Living without the performance is not easy.
It can feel raw, uncertain, exposed.
It can feel like standing without armor in a world that often
demands it.

But there is also a different kind of freedom:
The freedom of not wondering whether the love given is love for
the real self.
The freedom of not managing every interaction like a delicate
negotiation.
The freedom of no longer mistaking survival for living.

Being fully seen is not without cost.
But the cost of staying hidden is far greater.

When Sensitivity Becomes Self-Erasure

The Weight of Feeling Deeply

Sensitivity is often spoken of like a delicate thing.
A fragile temperament.
A quirk of personality.

But the truth is quieter and heavier than that.

Sensitivity, in its raw form, is not fragility.
It is depth.
The ability to feel beyond the surface.
The capacity to sense what others miss, to hold what others
drop, to notice what others dismiss.

It is not weakness.
It is a way of being that keeps the world vivid.

But in many spaces, this kind of feeling is treated like an
inconvenience.
Sensitivity becomes a problem to solve, a tendency to manage.
Strong feelings are framed as disruptions.
Intuitive insights are dismissed as overthinking.
Emotional reactions are seen as excess.

The message is absorbed early and often:
Feel less.
React less.

31

Want less.
Be less.

Sensitivity, when met with misunderstanding, is not nurtured.
It is discouraged.
Not through overt cruelty, but through subtle signals:
the way discomfort flickers across a face when a feeling is
shared,
the way a conversation grows strained when emotions deepen,
the way support is offered only when the messiness has been
cleaned up.

Over time, the weight of feeling deeply becomes harder to carry
—not because the feelings themselves are wrong, but because
there are so few places willing to hold them.

And so, many learn to carry their sensitivity alone.
Tucking it away.
Watering it down.
Dressing it up as something more acceptable.

Not because they stop feeling.
But because they stop believing it is safe to let those feelings be
seen.

How Sensitivity Turns Into Silence

Silence is rarely born from emptiness.
It is often born from too much fullness.
A fullness that has nowhere to go.

When sensitivity meets misunderstanding, it doesn't vanish.
It folds inward.
It retreats.

Not all at once.
Slowly.
A hesitation here.
A held breath there.
A decision, often unconscious, to withhold what feels too
complicated, too inconvenient, too much.

The silence that grows from sensitivity is not peaceful.
It is heavy.
It carries unsaid words and unfelt feelings.
It holds all the conversations that never found a home.

This kind of silence is not about choosing stillness.
It is about choosing survival.

It is a way of avoiding the risk that expression will be met with
dismissal or discomfort.
It is a way of avoiding the shame that can follow when deep
feelings are treated like mistakes.

The silence becomes a second skin.
Protective.
Restrictive.

It offers safety, but only the safety of invisibility.

To be sensitive in a world that rewards detachment often feels like standing in a room full of people speaking a language that refuses to name the things that matter most.
And so the sensitive learn to translate their experience into something quieter, simpler, safer.

Over time, the silence grows so familiar that breaking it feels dangerous.
Speaking honestly feels reckless.
Showing emotion feels exposed.
Wanting connection feels naive.

The silence is not emptiness.
It is a form of carrying everything alone.

The Invisible Loss

When sensitivity turns into silence, something subtle but profound is lost.
Not loudly.
Not dramatically.
More like erosion—the quiet wearing away of what once felt natural and alive.

It's not just the loss of words left unspoken.
It's the loss of being known.
The loss of being met in the places where feeling runs deep.
The loss of seeing oneself reflected in the understanding of another.

This kind of loss is difficult to name because there is nothing obvious to point to.
No clear rupture.
No visible wound.

Instead, there is a gradual fading.
The vibrant color of emotion dulled to shades that seem safer to show.
The sharp edges of longing worn down into something easier to carry alone.
The spontaneous gestures of care and connection tucked away before they can be misunderstood.

The loss is not only relational.
It is also internal.
Over time, there is a distance not just from others, but from the

self.
A gap between what is felt and what is expressed.
A disconnection between what is true and what is allowed to surface.

Many learn to live with this loss as if it is the price of maturity.
As if the quiet forfeiture of emotional honesty is a requirement for adulthood.

But underneath, the cost remains.
The cost of holding too much without sharing it.
The cost of appearing calm while carrying storms no one else can see.
The cost of trading real connection for the safer illusion of being easy to be around.

This loss does not scream.
It lingers.
It weighs.

And it waits—quietly—for the moment when the risk of staying hidden becomes greater than the risk of being seen.

Returning to the Unhidden Self

Returning begins not with speaking loudly, but with speaking at all.
It begins not with grand revelations, but with quiet acknowledgments.
A small truth allowed into a conversation.
A feeling named without apology.
A need admitted without softening its edges.

The work of returning to the unhidden self is slow because it asks for something forgotten:
Trust in the validity of what is felt.
Trust in the rightness of needing.
Trust that feeling deeply is not a flaw to correct but a signal to honor.

It requires dismantling the reflexes built for protection.
Reflexes that made silence feel safer than speech.
Reflexes that made shrinking feel safer than standing whole.

The risk of being misunderstood doesn't disappear.
The fear of discomfort doesn't evaporate.
But something else grows stronger—the quiet conviction that a life built on suppression is not the life that was meant to be lived.

Returning is not about demanding space.
It is about ceasing to negotiate for the right to exist fully.
It is about letting the self be seen without constant revision, without apology, without translation.

It does not happen all at once.
It happens in small, sometimes imperceptible shifts:
allowing a feeling to rise without rushing to quiet it,
staying present when discomfort threatens to close the heart,
choosing honesty even when it feels like the more dangerous
thing.

To return is to remember:
Sensitivity was never the problem.
Silence was never the solution.
Being fully here—fully feeling, fully present—is not too much.
It is the beginning of coming back to life.

Learning to Stay with the Ache

The Ache Beneath the Silence

There is an ache that lives beneath the silence.
Not the sharp, sudden kind that demands immediate attention,
but the quieter kind—the kind that settles in and stays.
The kind that becomes part of the background, present even
when forgotten.

It is not the ache of a single wound.
It is the accumulation of all the times feeling was swallowed
instead of spoken.
All the times need was hidden instead of shared.
All the times truth was softened, tucked away, or erased
altogether.

This ache is not easily named.
It doesn't always announce itself with tears or anger.
Often, it shows up as restlessness that lingers even in moments
of calm.
As a low hum of dissatisfaction in spaces that once felt full.
As an absence that no amount of company can seem to fill.

Many try to outrun this ache.
By staying busy.
By staying distracted.
By staying in motion.

But the ache is not something that can be outrun.
It is not something wrong to be fixed.
It is something true that has been waiting—patiently, quietly—for attention.

The ache beneath the silence is not a sign of failure.
It is not proof that something is broken.
It is evidence of all the life that has been carried, unspoken and unseen.

To feel this ache is not weakness.
It is the beginning of remembering that something has been missing.
And it is the first invitation to stop running.

Why We Resist the Ache

There are good reasons for resisting the ache.

Feeling it can seem dangerous.
Not because the ache itself will cause harm,
but because of what it threatens to reveal:
the weight of what has been carried,
the depth of what has been unsaid,
the memories tucked away to keep the days moving.

The ache holds more than sadness.
It holds the truths that were easier to avoid:
the longing for connection that went unmet,
the anger swallowed to keep peace,
the disappointments too persistent to voice.

To feel the ache fully means risking the collapse of all the
defenses carefully built.
The defense of busyness.
The defense of indifference.
The defense of pretending that needing less is strength.

There are stories told to justify the resistance.
Stories that say:
It's not so bad.
Other people have it worse.
This is just the way life is.

But these stories are not truth.
They are scaffolding—structures built to hold up a version of

living where nothing hurts too much, and nothing matters too deeply.

Resisting the ache can feel like survival.
And for a time, it may be.

But eventually, resistance hardens into something heavier than the ache itself.
A life of numbed-out routines.
Relationships without real connection.
Success that feels hollow even when achieved.

The ache, though uncomfortable, is honest.
It asks not for explanations, but for presence.
It asks not for solutions, but for attention.

The longer it is resisted, the louder it calls.

The Power of Staying

Staying with the ache is not about wallowing.
It is not about amplifying pain or chasing sorrow.
It is about refusing to abandon the parts of life that have been
quietly carrying what was too heavy to hold before.

There is a shift that happens when the ache is met without
resistance.
It does not vanish.
It does not explode.
It softens.
Not because the ache itself changes,
but because the posture toward it does.

When there is no longer a need to outrun or outwork it, the ache
reveals itself for what it truly is:
evidence of aliveness.

To feel it fully is to be reminded that there was never anything
wrong with needing, with longing, with hurting.
There was only the absence of places safe enough to hold it.

Staying requires courage—not the loud, declarative kind, but the
quieter courage of stillness.
The kind of courage that allows discomfort without flinching.
The kind that sits without rushing to explain, justify, or fix.

In the staying, something unexpected happens:
Grief begins to loosen its grip.
Anger finds its rightful voice.

Loneliness reveals not a defect, but a hunger for deeper connection.

The ache, once stayed with, stops feeling like a threat and starts feeling like a signal:
an invitation back to the parts of life that still wait to be lived fully.

Learning to Live with the Ache

Living with the ache does not mean giving up hope for joy.
It means learning that joy and ache can coexist.
That a life rich in feeling will make room for both.

The goal is not to eliminate the ache.
The goal is to carry it differently—
not as a burden to be hidden,
but as a companion that reminds the heart of its capacity.

Ache is not the opposite of healing.
It is often the first sign that healing is underway.
It means that what was silenced is finding its voice again.
It means that what was hidden is asking to be seen.

Living with the ache is a practice.
A daily choosing to stay open, even when closing would feel
easier.
A daily choosing to speak truth, even when silence would feel
safer.
A daily choosing to feel, even when feeling carries risk.

There will be days when the ache feels heavier.
Days when the old instincts—to numb, to rush, to shrink—will pull
hard.
But over time, staying becomes less about endurance and more
about presence.
Less about suffering and more about living honestly.

The ache may never disappear completely.
But neither does the strength learned from carrying it.
Neither does the clarity found on the other side of feeling what
once felt unbearable.

To live with the ache is to live fully awake—
to a life that holds sorrow and beauty,
loss and love,
pain and possibility.

It is not the easy way.
But it is the way home.

The Shape of What Was Denied

What We Were Told Not to Be

Before learning who to become, many first learn who not to be.

The messages are rarely direct.
They are absorbed in small gestures, glances, silences.
The discomfort in a parent's face when emotion rises too high.
The laughter that cuts too sharply when vulnerability spills into the open.
The tightening of space around anger, sadness, or uncontained joy.

Over time, these signals accumulate into a map of the unacceptable.
Too loud.
Too sensitive.
Too complicated.
Too demanding.

What is denied is not random.
It is often the parts of the self that are most alive—
the parts that want too much,
feel too deeply,
long too intensely,
question too insistently.

Rather than being welcomed, these parts are trained into silence.
Not through force, but through repetition:
the repeated suggestion that what feels natural is excessive,
that what feels true is inconvenient.

Many learn to edit themselves before they fully understand what
they are erasing.
They learn to shrink desires into something more manageable.
They learn to soften anger into irritation.
They learn to tuck away the wildness that once made them
unmistakably alive.

The shape of what is denied does not disappear.
It lives quietly at the edges,
waiting for a time when it will be safe enough to be seen again.

But before that time comes, many learn to live without it—
to navigate the world with a self carefully trimmed to fit into
spaces too small for the whole truth.

The Unlived Life

Living without the denied parts of the self often looks, from the outside, like adaptation.
It looks like composure, success, discipline.

It looks like someone who has figured out how to navigate the world with minimal disruption.
Someone who doesn't ask for too much.
Someone who doesn't take up more space than is offered.
Someone who seems, in every visible way, fine.

But there is a difference between living and managing.
Between being alive and being accommodated.

Without the parts of the self that have been denied, life becomes narrower.
Dreams shrink to what feels practical.
Relationships flatten to what feels predictable.
Conversations skim across the surface where it is safest.

The unlived life is not empty—it is crowded with compromises.
Not conscious, deliberate choices, but quiet negotiations made to avoid discomfort:
avoiding vulnerability to prevent rejection,
avoiding ambition to prevent disappointment,
avoiding real feeling to prevent the risk of being overwhelmed.

The unlived life carries a particular ache:
the sense that something essential has been set aside but cannot be forgotten.

It lingers in moments of success that feel hollow.
It echoes in relationships that feel safe but not real.
It hums beneath achievements that do not satisfy.

It is the weight of all the parts that were denied still waiting at the edges,
still holding the shape of the life that could have been lived—
not perfect, not without pain,
but whole.

The Quiet Grief

Grief does not always announce itself with tears or goodbyes.
Sometimes, it arrives more quietly—
a dull ache beneath the rhythms of everyday life,
a vague sense of absence that cannot be easily named.

The grief of the unlived life is not for what was taken away by others,
but for what was slowly set aside by the self,
piece by piece,
over years of trying to be acceptable.

It is grief for the desires that were never spoken aloud.
For the anger that was muted into silence.
For the joy that was rationed into smaller, safer expressions.
For the tenderness that was hidden away to protect it from being misunderstood.

This kind of grief has no clear beginning.
No sharp moment to point to.
It builds in the background,
layered into the choices made for safety,
the opportunities turned down for fear of being seen too fully.

Often, it is hard to recognize this grief for what it is.
It can feel like dissatisfaction.
Like restlessness.
Like loneliness that persists even in connection.

But underneath, it is the simple sorrow of a life lived without all of its available colors.
A life edited for the comfort of others.
A life that learned to apologize for its own intensity before it had the chance to explore it.

Grieving what was denied is not indulgence.
It is honesty.
It is the first step in acknowledging that something important was given up along the way—
not out of weakness,
but out of the human need for belonging.

And once this grief is named,
it no longer needs to be carried alone or in silence.

Reclaiming What Remains

What was denied is not destroyed.
What was set aside is not lost beyond reach.

It waits—
quietly, patiently—
beneath the layers of survival and silence.

Reclaiming these parts is not a matter of force or urgency.
It is not about undoing the past with grand declarations.
It is about learning to listen again.
To the small voice that never fully left.
To the instincts that still flicker beneath caution.
To the longings that surface in moments of unexpected stillness.

Reclaiming is slow work.
It asks for tenderness,
for patience with all that was hidden for good reason.

It begins with noticing where the self shrinks out of habit.
Where words are softened unnecessarily.
Where emotions are edited mid-sentence.
Where dreams are downsized before they have the chance to be
spoken aloud.

It continues with choosing—
Choosing to speak a little more plainly.
Choosing to want a little more honestly.
Choosing to stay with feeling a little longer before tucking it away.

The parts once denied are not problems to solve.
They are invitations—
back to a fuller, more honest life.

A life where joy is not rationed.
Where sadness is not disguised.
Where love is not negotiated down to something easier to hold.
Where the self is not portioned out in acceptable doses.

Reclaiming what remains is not about becoming someone new.
It is about becoming fully what was always there—
waiting not for permission,
but for recognition.

Need is Not Weakness

The Shame Around Needing

Many grow up learning that need is dangerous.
Not because anyone says it outright,
but because of how needs are met—with discomfort, with
withdrawal, with disappointment.

Over time, a quiet lesson settles in:
needing less is safer.
Needing less makes connection easier.
Needing less protects against rejection.

The world often rewards the appearance of self-sufficiency.
Praises the ones who ask for nothing.
Admires the ones who seem invulnerable, invincible.

And so, needing becomes something to hide.
Something to be ashamed of.
A private source of discomfort, tucked away behind smiles and
composure.

But the shame around needing is not natural.
It is learned.
Learned in moments when vulnerability was met with dismissal.
Learned in moments when asking led to disappointment.
Learned in moments when wanting more cost more than silence.

This shame teaches many to view needs not as natural
expressions of being human,
but as flaws to be corrected,
weaknesses to be managed,
embarrassments to be disguised.

Yet the presence of need is not a failure of character.
It is a sign of life.
A signal that connection matters, that fulfillment matters, that
living fully requires more than endurance.

Shame tries to convince otherwise.
But shame, however convincing it may seem, is not truth.
It is only the residue of experiences that said it was safer not to
ask at all.

How Need Got Mistranslated

Need, in its original form, is simple.
It is the body asking for what sustains it.
It is the heart reaching toward what makes life more bearable,
more whole.

But over time, many learn to mistranslate need into something
else.
Into desperation.
Into dependency.
Into weakness.

This mistranslation is not accidental.
It often begins in environments where needing more than what is
offered feels like an inconvenience.
Where reaching out results not in support, but in disappointment.
Where emotional hunger is met with silence or rejection.

The body, learning this, adapts.
It begins to hide its needs beneath other things:
Ambition that masks longing.
Independence that masks hurt.
Caregiving that masks the hope of being cared for.

Need itself does not disappear.
It finds other languages when the original one is not welcomed.

Sometimes it shows up in overwork, in the constant reaching for
achievement to fill what connection has not.
Sometimes it shows up in relationships, in the unspoken

expectation that others should intuit what cannot be safely asked for.
Sometimes it shows up in withdrawal, in the quiet belief that needing nothing is the safest way to avoid disappointment.

The mistranslation is subtle but powerful.
It teaches that needing is dangerous, not because need is wrong, but because past experiences made it costly.

And yet, beneath all the layers, the original language of need remains.
Unspoiled.
Unashamed.
Waiting to be remembered.

Relearning the Language of Need

Relearning how to need openly is not about becoming helpless.
It is about returning to a more honest way of living.

It begins with noticing where need has been hidden—
where silence has taken the place of asking,
where over-functioning has taken the place of vulnerability,
where withdrawal has taken the place of reaching out.

Relearning starts small.
It starts with the quiet permission to admit, even internally,
I want.
I miss.
I hope.

It continues with the practice of expression—
not masked by apology or softened into half-requests,
but spoken plainly and clearly.

It requires unlearning the idea that needing is a burden.
Unlearning the idea that asking is a form of weakness.
Unlearning the belief that self-sufficiency is the highest form of
strength.

Strength is not the absence of need.
Strength is the willingness to acknowledge what is human,
to bring needs into the light,
to trust that real connection begins where pretense ends.

Relearning the language of need is slow work.
It asks for patience.

It asks for tenderness toward the reflexes built to protect the self
from disappointment.
It asks for trust—
not that every need will be met exactly as hoped,
but that the act of naming them is in itself a return to dignity.

The Strength in Needing

There is a particular strength in allowing need to be seen.
Not a performative strength,
but a quieter, deeper kind—
the kind built on honesty rather than image.

It takes strength to resist the pull of self-erasure.
To refuse the old habit of pretending everything is fine.
To stand in the discomfort of asking without the guarantee of
receiving.

It takes strength to believe that needs are not a threat to
connection,
but the very foundation of it.
To trust that being real is more valuable than being easy.
To risk vulnerability in a world that often rewards detachment.

Needing is not the problem.
Needing is the signal that life is still moving through the body,
that connection still matters,
that the heart has not gone silent.

The strength in needing is not measured by whether needs are
always met.
It is measured by the willingness to bring them into the light,
to honor them without shame,
to let them shape a life that is not built on pretending.

To need is to be human.
To acknowledge need is to reclaim what was never wrong—only misunderstood.

And in that reclamation,
there is not weakness,
but a return to a kind of wholeness that no performance can replicate.

Loneliness That Tells the Truth

Loneliness That Isn't About Being Alone

Loneliness is often misunderstood.
It is seen as a matter of numbers—how many friends, how full
the calendar, how busy the life.

But loneliness is rarely about being alone.
It is about being unseen.
It is about the quiet ache that lingers even in rooms filled with
conversation.
It is about feeling unknown, even by the people closest.

There can be noise and still no real connection.
There can be laughter and still a hollow space inside.
There can be hands held and still a distance that words cannot
cross.

This kind of loneliness is not solved by proximity.
It is not solved by more gatherings, more messages, more
movement.

It is a deeper loneliness—
the loneliness of a self hidden behind careful performances,
the loneliness of being half-present out of habit,
the loneliness of being praised for the very invisibility that aches
to be undone.

This loneliness tells a quieter truth:
that company is not the same as connection,
that being liked is not the same as being known,
that being included is not the same as being understood.

It tells the truth that presence alone cannot heal what hiding has
hollowed out.

The remedy is not more people, more noise, more doing.
The remedy begins with recognition—
recognizing that real belonging cannot be negotiated through
self-erasure.

The Sacred Space of Not-Being-Chosen

There is a particular sting in not being chosen.
It can feel like failure.
It can feel like proof that something essential is missing, broken,
unworthy.

But not being chosen can also reveal something quieter, harder
to see:
the places where compromise has been refused,
the spaces where performance has been set down,
the boundaries that have been drawn not for punishment, but for
preservation.

There is a sacredness in this space—
not because loneliness itself is sacred,
but because what it protects can be.

Not being chosen creates an opening.
An opening where the self, no longer edited for acceptance, can
breathe.
An opening where the absence of applause makes it easier to
hear the sound of one's own life.

It is in this space that honesty can surface.
Not the honesty crafted for comfort,
but the honesty that says:
This is who I am without explanation.
This is what I need without apology.

The world often treats not being chosen as something to be fixed,
as a flaw to correct,
as a gap to fill.

But not every silence is emptiness.
Not every absence is lack.
Some silences are space being cleared for what can only grow
without the weight of constant approval.

In the sacred space of not-being-chosen, there is an invitation:
an invitation to belong first to the self,
an invitation to become whole without the need to fit.

Loneliness vs. Self-Abandonment

Loneliness is often seen as something done to us—
the result of absence, distance, exclusion.

But there is a deeper, quieter loneliness that does not come from
the outside.
It comes from the slow drift away from the self.
From the choices made to be accepted rather than known.
From the performances given not for connection, but for survival.

This is not simply loneliness.
This is self-abandonment.

Self-abandonment happens in small, almost invisible ways:
Laughing when something isn't funny.
Agreeing when the heart resists.
Shrinking a truth into something palatable.
Silencing a need before it reaches the surface.

Over time, these small departures accumulate.
And the loneliness that results is not about missing other people.
It is about missing the parts of the self that were left behind to
maintain the illusion of belonging.

Self-abandonment teaches that staying close to others is more
important than staying close to oneself.
That being accepted is worth the cost of being honest.
That peace purchased through silence is safer than conflict born
of truth.

But the loneliness that follows is sharp.
It is the loneliness of being unseen not by others,
but by the self.

Loneliness and self-abandonment are not the same.
Loneliness can be endured.
Self-abandonment hollows.

To heal from this kind of loneliness is not to find more people,
but to find the courage to stop leaving oneself behind.

What Comes Through the Silence

Silence, once feared, can become something else.
Not a void to escape,
but a space where something real begins to surface.

When the noise of performance fades,
when the scramble for approval stills,
when the need to be chosen is set down—
what remains is a different kind of presence.

In this silence, the self begins to speak again.
Not loudly.
Not urgently.
But steadily.

First, in small ways:
A feeling acknowledged without judgment.
A desire allowed without apology.
A boundary held without explanation.

Then, in larger ones:
A trust in the body's signals.
A loyalty to the heart's knowing.
A patience for the slow unfolding of what is true.

Through the silence, grief may come.
So may anger, regret, tenderness.
All the emotions set aside in the pursuit of being acceptable may
rise to the surface, asking not for control but for witness.

And with them comes something else:
Clarity.

Clarity about what was lost and what can be reclaimed.
Clarity about what connection really requires—
not perfection,
but presence.
Not shape-shifting,
but staying.

What comes through the silence is not just the memory of who
was once abandoned.
It is the beginning of coming home—
not to others,
but to oneself.

Grieving the Edited Self

The Mourning We Avoid

There is a kind of mourning that often goes unnamed.
Not for someone lost,
but for the version of the self left behind along the way.

This mourning is quiet.
It moves beneath the surface of achievement,
beneath the celebrations of success,
beneath the daily rituals of being "fine."

It is the mourning for the parts of life unlived.
For the instincts silenced.
For the dreams downsized.
For the truths softened into something more acceptable.

It is mourning for the full voice that was never fully heard.
For the desires dismissed too soon.
For the boldness dulled by fear of being too much.

This kind of grief is easy to avoid.
Easy to rationalize away with stories about timing, about
circumstance, about realism.
Easy to bury beneath busyness,
beneath new goals,
beneath the relentless pursuit of proving something—to whom,
it's hard to say.

But avoidance does not erase mourning.
It only delays it.
It turns it into a low, constant hum—
an ache that no amount of success can silence.

To grieve the edited self is not self-indulgence.
It is not weakness.

It is a reckoning.
A recognition that a life shaped around absence is not the same
as a life fully lived.
It is the first step toward reclaiming what was once surrendered
in the name of being acceptable, agreeable, survivable.

What It Means to Finally Say "I Miss Me"

There is a particular power in the moment when a person can
say, without bitterness or blame:
I miss me.

Not the curated version of the self built for approval.
Not the careful image constructed for acceptance.
But the self that existed before the shrinking began—
before the edits, the silences, the compromises.

To say *I miss me* is not an accusation.
It is not a condemnation of the paths taken or the survival
strategies once needed.

It is an acknowledgment:
that somewhere along the way, something essential was set
aside.
That survival cost more than was ever expected.
That belonging came at the price of authenticity.

I miss me is not a rejection of the life built around adaptation.
It is the recognition that what was lost matters.
That the instincts muted for safety were not flaws.
That the feelings softened to keep peace were not mistakes.
That the desires hidden away were not shameful, but sacred.

This admission is not easy.
It strips away the comfort of denial.
It asks for the courage to sit with absence without rushing to fill it.

But in this mourning, there is also a kind of homecoming.
A return to the self not as it was imagined to be,
but as it always was beneath the edits:
untidy, earnest, whole.

To say *I miss me* is to begin again—
not by discarding what has been lived,
but by daring to retrieve what was never truly lost,
only waiting to be remembered.

Letting Go of Personas You Built to Survive

Personas are built carefully, even when the building is unconscious.
They are shaped from the small, daily decisions to be more acceptable, more manageable, more praised.

The easygoing one.
The high-achiever.
The caretaker.
The one who never needs too much.

These personas are not deceptions.
They are protections—crafted to survive environments that could not welcome the full truth of who was underneath.

They served a purpose.
They kept connection within reach when real belonging felt too risky.
They kept the self hidden enough to stay safe.

But what protects can also imprison.
Over time, the persona can become so familiar that it feels indistinguishable from identity.
The distance between who is lived and who is real grows harder to see.

Letting go of these personas is not betrayal.
It is not a rejection of what was needed to survive.
It is a quiet acknowledgment that survival is not the only goal anymore.

To let go is not to erase the past,
but to loosen the grip of the old strategies.
To allow the self to step out from behind the armor.
To trust that the parts once hidden can live without constant
protection.

It is slow work.
It requires patience, tenderness, a willingness to grieve not just
what was lost, but what was necessary.

The personas do not vanish overnight.
They soften, they fall away, they dissolve—
not through force, but through a steady refusal to pretend any
longer.

And what remains is not a failure.
It is a return.

Rituals for Reentry into Your Truth

Reentry into the whole self does not happen in a single act.
It is not a grand declaration or a one-time decision.
It is a practice—
a quiet, persistent return to what feels honest, even when
honesty feels unfamiliar.

Small rituals mark the way.

Speaking the full truth in a conversation, even if the voice
shakes.
Allowing a no to stand without explanation.
Letting joy take up space without apology.
Sitting with sadness without trying to translate it into something
easier to carry.

These rituals are not performances for others to see.
They are intimate agreements with the self:
to stay present,
to stay honest,
to stay whole.

Reentry asks for attention to what feels alive and what feels
rehearsed.
It asks for the courage to disappoint others in the service of no
longer disappointing oneself.
It asks for tenderness toward the parts still tempted to edit, to
shrink, to retreat.

It is not about perfection.
It is about practice.
It is about noticing the moments when the old persona wants to step in and choosing, gently, to stay real instead.

Rituals of reentry are small, almost imperceptible at first.
But over time, they weave a different kind of life—
a life that does not require constant vigilance,
a life that holds both vulnerability and strength without contradiction,
a life that can bear the full weight of truth without collapse.

This is not a return to who was before the edits.
It is a return to someone wiser, braver—
someone who knows what it costs to leave the self behind,
and chooses, now, to stay.

Anger as Sacred Fire

Why Anger Was Never the Enemy

Anger has long been misunderstood.
Taught to be feared, managed, suppressed.
Treated as a problem to solve rather than a signal to heed.

For many, anger is seen as dangerous—
a loss of control,
a rupture of relationships,
a threat to belonging.

But anger, in its truest form, is not chaos.
It is clarity.

Anger names what is intolerable.
It draws the line where harm begins.
It speaks the truth that polite silence cannot carry.

When anger is denied, something vital is lost:
the ability to recognize when boundaries have been crossed,
the ability to stand in defense of the self,
the ability to say: *This is not acceptable.*
This must change.

The enemy is not anger.
The enemy is what happens when anger is disowned,
when it is forced underground where it festers,

grows distorted,
erupts without warning.

Anger, welcomed and understood, is not destructive.
It is instructive.
It is a sacred fire—
capable not only of burning down what harms,
but of lighting the way to what heals.

Reclaiming anger is not about giving it free reign.
It is about giving it rightful place.
It is about trusting that anger, like any sacred force, can be
powerful without being reckless.

Clean Fire vs. Scorched Earth

Not all expressions of anger are the same.
Some burn clean.
Others burn everything down.

Clean fire is anger honored without distortion.
It is anger that speaks without needing to scream.
It is anger that holds its ground without seeking to wound.
It is anger that clarifies without destroying.

Clean fire rises from presence, not panic.
It comes from staying close to the truth rather than being
overtaken by it.
It protects boundaries without punishing.
It names harm without replicating it.

Scorched earth, by contrast, is anger exiled too long.
It is anger that, denied and suppressed, turns volatile.
It lashes out not to heal, but to hurt.
It leaves devastation in its wake—relationships broken, trust
shattered, self-respect eroded.

Scorched earth is anger that forgot its sacredness.

The difference is not in the intensity of feeling,
but in the posture toward it.

Clean fire says:
*This is not okay—and I will stand in that truth with clarity and
care.*

Scorched earth says:
This is not okay—and everything must pay for it.

The work is not to fear anger,
but to learn to carry it cleanly.
To allow it space without letting it overrun.
To let it inform without letting it consume.

Clean fire is anger held in hands that know its worth.
It burns brightly, but with purpose—
clearing what no longer serves,
making space for something stronger, truer, more whole.

Making Space for Rage Without Becoming It

Rage, when it arrives, can feel total.
It can fill the body,
consume the breath,
crowd out reason.

It is tempting to believe that feeling rage fully will mean becoming
it—
that to allow it space is to surrender control.

But feeling is not the same as becoming.
Feeling is presence.
Becoming is possession.

There is a difference between allowing rage to move through
and letting it take over.
There is a difference between honoring rage as real
and mistaking it for the whole truth.

Making space for rage means refusing to exile it,
but also refusing to be swallowed by it.
It means learning to hold the heat without letting it burn through
everything.
It means staying present even when the body surges and the
heart pounds.

This is not about repression.
Repression drives rage underground where it festers,
where it twists into bitterness and resentment.

Nor is it about indulgence.
Indulgence feeds rage until it is all that remains,
leaving wreckage where there should have been repair.

Making space is something quieter:
a deep breath when the impulse is to lash out,
a pause when the urge is to punish,
a hand placed gently over the heart as if to say:
I see you. I hear you. I will not abandon you.

Rage does not need to be feared.
It needs to be witnessed.
It needs to be given room to speak—
not to dictate,
but to tell its part of the story.

And when rage is honored without being obeyed,
it becomes what it was meant to be all along:
a messenger,
a protector,
a sacred fire guiding the way back to what must be defended.

Transmuting Fury into Fierce Clarity

Fury, left unattended, can devour.
But fury, honored and listened to, can be transmuted.
Not erased.
Not denied.
Transformed.

The transformation does not happen by suppressing the force of anger.
It happens by refining it.
By asking:
What truth is this fire pointing toward?
What boundary needs to be honored?
What needs to be rebuilt, reimagined, reclaimed?

Fury is the raw material.
Clarity is what can be forged from it.

When fury is met with presence,
when it is neither fed nor feared,
it sharpens into something fierce but steady.

Not the chaos of retaliation,
but the calm of resolve.
Not the noise of vengeance,
but the quiet certainty that says:
This is where I stand.
This is what I will no longer carry.
This is what will not be allowed to continue.

Transmuting fury into clarity asks for patience.
It asks for the willingness to sit in discomfort without rushing to
act.
It asks for trust—
trust that the fire, if tended, will not destroy,
but will illuminate.

Fierce clarity does not need to shout.
It does not need to threaten.
It simply *is*—unshakable, undeniable, rooted.

This is the sacred work of anger.
Not to consume, but to clear.
Not to punish, but to protect.
Not to destroy, but to declare, with steady hands and an open
heart:
I am no longer available for harm.
I am no longer willing to abandon myself for peace.
I am still here—and this fire keeps me whole.

Saying No Without Explaining Why

The Addiction to Justification

There is a subtle, persistent pull to explain every boundary.
To soften every no.
To dress refusals in reasons that will make them more palatable.

This pull is not born of malice.
It grows from years of learning that approval is tied to agreement,
that saying no is not just a denial,
but a disruption.

And so many become fluent in justification:
stacking reasons to make the no sound reasonable,
piling on context to make the boundary seem fair,
softening the truth until it almost sounds like a yes.

Justification becomes a reflex—
an attempt to control the response,
to preempt disappointment,
to avoid being seen as difficult or selfish.

But justification costs more than it protects.
It leaks power.
It turns boundaries into negotiations.
It teaches others to believe that permission to say no must be
earned.

No is a complete sentence.
Not because it is easy,
but because it is honest.

The addiction to justification is understandable.
But it is not necessary.

Freedom begins when no longer explaining becomes an act of
trust—
trust in the boundary,
trust in the self,
trust that others' discomfort is not a reason to abandon what is
true.

No Is a Full Sentence

No is often treated as incomplete.
As if it must be followed by an explanation,
an apology,
a justification.

But no, in its fullness, needs nothing added to it.
No stands on its own.

No says:
This is where I end and you begin.
This is what I have the capacity for.
This is what I choose to honor within myself.

No is not cruelty.
No is not disrespect.
No is not rejection of another's worth.

It is a simple statement of truth.
A marker of self-respect.
A declaration that boundaries are not barriers to love, but
containers for it.

When no is allowed to stand without adornment, something
shifts.
Self-respect deepens.
Trust in one's own limits grows stronger.
Connection, though fewer, becomes truer—built not on
performance, but on honesty.

No is a full sentence because the self is a full being.
Not an apology waiting to be spoken.
Not a compromise waiting to be made.
Not an explanation waiting to be justified.

Practicing no without explanation is not about being rigid.
It is about being clear.

It is a quiet revolution:
choosing truth over performance,
clarity over approval,
integrity over ease.

The Power of Silence After "No"

There is a particular discomfort in the silence that follows a no.
A tension.
A space where expectation hangs in the air,
waiting for something more.

An explanation.
A softening.
A way out.

But the silence after no is not empty.
It is potent.

It is the place where the boundary takes shape.
Where the truth settles.
Where both people are invited to sit with what is real rather than
what is rehearsed.

Filling the silence is tempting.
It feels easier to explain than to endure discomfort.
It feels safer to talk than to trust.

But the silence holds a power that words cannot.
It communicates:
This no is not a negotiation.
This boundary is not a debate.
This truth is not fragile.

Silence after no is not aggression.
It is not passive resistance.
It is clarity, left unclouded by apology or over-explanation.

It is an act of respect:
respect for the self,
respect for the boundary,
respect for the possibility that real connection can survive
honesty.

The power of silence is not in how loudly it speaks,
but in how steadily it stands.

It says:
I will not abandon my truth to ease your discomfort.
I will not rush to soften what needs to stay firm.
I trust you to handle my boundary—or to step away from it.

And in that trust, something deeper is offered:
the possibility of connection built not on performance,
but on presence.

Who Leaves When You Set a Boundary—and Why That's a Gift

Not everyone will stay when the boundaries are no longer blurred.
Not everyone will remain when the yes is no longer automatic,
when the smile is no longer guaranteed,
when the silence is no longer offered as comfort.

Some will leave.

They will leave not because of cruelty,
but because the terms of engagement have changed.
The old agreements—spoken or unspoken—
that comfort would come at the cost of honesty,
that peace would come at the price of self-abandonment—
are no longer being upheld.

Boundaries reveal what words often hide.
They clarify who is willing to meet the real self—
not the accommodating version,
not the edited version,
but the whole, complex, untidy self.

Who leaves when a boundary is set is not random.
It is instructive.

Those who leave are often those who were more connected to
the benefits of the boundary-less self than to the truth of the full
self.

Those who expected compliance as proof of loyalty.
Those who mistook silence for kindness, and endurance for love.

Their leaving is not a failure.
It is a gift.

It clears space for those who are capable of meeting the unedited self.
It opens room for relationships built on respect, not convenience.
It makes way for connection that does not require shrinking.

Boundaries are not walls.
They are invitations—
invitations to come closer with honesty,
or to step away with respect.

And who stays, who chooses to lean in rather than turn away,
will be those who understand that boundaries are not rejections
—

they are revelations.

When You're Finally Willing to Lose Them

The Fear of Being Alone vs. the Cost of Being Half-Seen

The fear of being alone is powerful.
It can shape choices quietly,
convincing many to stay where they are only partially seen,
partially known,
partially met.

The fear is understandable.
Aloneness is often portrayed as failure,
as proof that something essential has gone wrong.

But there is a cost to being half-seen.
A cost that accrues slowly—
the cost of silencing truths to stay agreeable,
of shrinking desires to avoid disruption,
of camouflaging real feelings to maintain peace.

The fear of being alone asks:
What if no one else comes?
What if this is as good as it gets?

But the cost of being half-seen asks a different question:
What parts of the self must be abandoned to stay here?
What becomes of a life lived in half-light, half-truth, half-presence?

Over time, the cost becomes heavier than the fear.

And when the cost is finally acknowledged,
a different kind of fear rises—
not the fear of being alone,
but the fear of losing the self in order not to be.

This is where the reckoning begins:
a recognition that being alone is hard,
but being unseen is harder.

The risk of solitude holds pain.
But the pain of perpetual partialness
is the slow erosion of what it means to be whole.

Leaving People Who Can't Meet the Real You

Leaving is not always dramatic.
It is not always a slammed door or a final confrontation.

Sometimes it is quieter—
a slow, deliberate stepping away from spaces where the self has
been edited too often,
too carefully,
for too long.

Leaving people who can't meet the real self is not an act of
cruelty.
It is an act of self-loyalty.

It is the acknowledgment that proximity without presence is not
connection.
That being tolerated is not the same as being loved.
That being half-understood is not the same as being seen.

Leaving does not mean there is no love.
It means that love, when it costs authenticity, asks too high a
price.

It means recognizing when conversations have become
performances,
when connection feels like an agreement to be less,
when care is conditional upon remaining palatable, manageable,
small.

Leaving is a risk.
It invites loneliness.
It opens the door to uncertainty.

But it also creates space.
Space for relationships that do not require contortion.
Space for belonging that does not demand betrayal of the self.
Space for love that can hold the real, the messy, the full.

It is not the absence of others that marks true loneliness.
It is the absence of self.

And leaving those who cannot meet the real self
is not abandoning them—
it is refusing to abandon what has been fought for:
the right to be whole.

You're Not Failing—You're Recalibrating

It's easy to mistake departure for failure.
Easy to believe that walking away is proof of brokenness,
proof that something was missing,
proof that something was wrong.

But leaving is not failing.
It is recalibrating.

It is adjusting a life built around surviving toward a life built
around living.
It is recognizing that the cost of staying has become too high—
not just emotionally,
but existentially.

Recalibrating is an act of precision:
choosing to realign with truth over comfort,
authenticity over approval,
wholeness over performance.

It requires the courage to look clearly at what connection has
become:
a negotiation rather than a meeting,
an endurance test rather than a sanctuary,
a performance rather than a homecoming.

Leaving is not the abandonment of hope.
It is the refusal to keep hoping in places where hope has become
hostage to half-visibility.

Recalibrating does not happen all at once.
It is slow.
It is deliberate.
It is a series of small, steady choices to move closer to a life
where the self does not have to shrink to belong.

There will be moments of doubt.
Moments where the silence feels louder than the connection ever
did.
Moments where the absence feels heavier than the compromise.

But recalibration is not about immediate comfort.
It is about lasting alignment.

And alignment begins not with being chosen,
but with choosing oneself.

The Exhale of Letting Go

Letting go is not always a moment of triumph.
Sometimes it is quieter—
a slow, steady release of what was once clung to out of fear,
habit, or hope.

It is not a loud departure.
It is a deep exhale.

The exhale of no longer explaining.
No longer contorting.
No longer waiting for recognition in places unwilling to offer it.

The exhale is not the absence of grief.
Grief is there—inevitable, necessary.
But alongside it, there is something else:
relief.

Relief in the space that opens when the weight of performance is
set down.
Relief in the stillness that follows the end of striving to be
understood by those committed to misunderstanding.
Relief in the quiet knowing that the self no longer has to be
bartered for love.

Letting go is not a rejection of the past.
It is an acceptance that not everything or everyone is meant to
come with us into what's next.

Some connections are seasonal.
Some relationships are chapters, not lifetimes.

The exhale of letting go makes room for new breath, new life,
new connection—
not connections dependent on shrinking,
but connections rooted in staying fully, unapologetically whole.

The exhale is not defeat.
It is liberation.

A soft but certain return to the self,
to the body,
to the life that no longer requires explaining,
defending,
or dimming.

Wholeness Isn't Always Pretty

Healing Doesn't Make You Saintly

Healing is often wrapped in language that suggests perfection—
as if becoming whole means becoming gentle, serene,
untouchable by anger or grief.

But healing doesn't make anyone saintly.
It doesn't erase the messy parts.
It doesn't dissolve frustration, or eliminate sorrow, or remove the
sharp edges of human feeling.

Healing doesn't turn a person into a monument of peace.
It turns a person into someone more honest—
honest about hurt,
honest about limits,
honest about the fact that growth does not mean immunity to
pain.

The work of healing is not about becoming someone flawless.
It's about becoming someone real.

It's about living with the contradictions—
feeling strong and still uncertain,
feeling grateful and still grieving,
feeling loving and still needing space.

Healing doesn't smooth everything over.
It exposes what was hidden.
It demands the courage to stay present with what still stings,
to tell the truth about what still struggles to be soft.

To heal is to become less performative, not more polished.
It is to allow the self to be complicated, contradictory, alive.

Saintliness was never the goal.
Sanctity was never the destination.

Wholeness is not about transcending human messiness—
it is about reclaiming the right to be fully human without apology.

You're Allowed to Be Messy and Still Growing

Growth is not tidy.
It does not move in straight lines.
It is not a steady ascent toward a polished, perfected self.

Growth is wild.
It surges forward and pulls back.
It blooms and wilts and blooms again.
It stumbles, backtracks, doubts, begins again.

There is a myth that growing means becoming more controlled,
more polished,
more admirable.

But growth often looks like mess—
like breaking old patterns and falling into them again.
Like knowing better and not always doing better.
Like learning and forgetting and relearning what was already
known.

The mess is not failure.
It is evidence of movement.
It is proof that life is still being engaged fully,
not from a safe distance,
but from inside the discomfort of real change.

You are allowed to be messy and still growing.
You are allowed to have bad days and still be healing.
You are allowed to feel lost and still be finding your way.

Growth doesn't require perfection.
It only asks for presence.

It asks for the courage to stay engaged with life,
even when it's confusing,
even when it's hard to recognize progress,
even when the mess feels larger than the movement.

The measure of growth is not in how clean the journey looks.
It is in how honestly it is lived.

Being Seen Requires Being Honest, Not Perfect

Visibility is often mistaken for exposure.
For being polished, prepared, packaged.
For presenting a version of the self that can be admired without discomfort.

But real visibility—the kind that allows for true connection—
requires something different.
It requires honesty.

Not the curated honesty of what is safe to share,
but the unvarnished honesty of being seen in process,
in uncertainty,
in complexity.

Perfection creates distance.
It invites admiration, maybe,
but not intimacy.
Not real knowing.
Not the kind of connection that can hold the weight of a whole life.

Honesty does what perfection cannot.
It opens a door.
It offers an invitation:
Come closer, if you can hold this.
Come closer, if you can sit with what is real and unfinished and true.

Being seen honestly asks for courage.
The courage to let others witness the parts still in flux.

The courage to allow love to find the real self,
not the rehearsed one.

It is a risk.
Some will prefer the polish.
Some will withdraw from the unedited parts.
Some will not know how to stay when the illusion of perfection
dissolves.

But those who can stay—
those who meet honesty with their own—
create the kind of connection that cannot be built on image.

Being seen does not require being perfect.
It requires being willing to stand, even trembling,
in the light of what is true.

A Life That Can Hold All of You

Wholeness is not about fixing what's broken.
It is about creating a life that can hold all of it—
the beauty and the bruises,
the wisdom and the wounds,
the strength and the softness.

It is not about silencing the parts that still hurt,
nor exalting only the parts that shine.
It is about allowing every piece to have a place at the table—
not because every piece is equally easy to love,
but because every piece is part of the truth.

A life that can hold all of you is not one that demands constant
self-improvement.
It is one that allows for self-acceptance.
It is one that understands that wholeness is not the absence of
struggle,
but the ability to live without needing to divide the self into
acceptable and unacceptable parts.

This life is not built by accident.
It is built by deliberate choice:
choosing presence over perfection,
choosing honesty over image,
choosing compassion over critique.

It is built by refusing to exile the parts of the self that do not fit
someone else's idea of who you should be.

It is built by trusting that a full life—
a life that can hold rage and tenderness,
grief and gratitude,
uncertainty and conviction—
is richer than a perfect one.

A life that can hold all of you is not a life without fear,
but a life where fear does not have the final word.

It is not a life free of mess,
but a life brave enough to welcome it.

It is not a life without ache,
but a life wide enough to let the ache be part of the music.

It is, finally, a life that feels like home—
not because it is easy,
but because it is true.

Reclaiming the Right to Take Up Space

Body, Voice, Presence: The Trifecta of Return

Taking up space is not just about volume.
It is not only about speaking louder or standing taller.
It is about a deeper return—
a reclamation of what was once softened, hidden, made smaller.

The return begins in the body.
In the decision to inhabit it fully,
to walk without apology,
to stand without shrinking.
To live not at the edges of the self,
but at the center.

It continues in the voice.
Not in shouting,
but in allowing what is true to be said plainly.
Allowing desire to be voiced without dilution,
allowing no to be spoken without cushioning,
allowing celebration to sound without restraint.

And it lives in presence.
In showing up without deflecting,
without minimizing,
without explaining away existence as if permission is needed to
be here at all.

111

Body.
Voice.
Presence.

The trifecta of return.

Not return to a version of the self others prefer,
but return to the self that was never meant to shrink.

Reclaiming space is not about domination.
It is not about crowding others out.
It is about ending the quiet war against the right to exist fully,
visibly,
unapologetically.

This is the work:
to come back into the body without flinching,
into the voice without softening,
into presence without apology.

This is the return.

From Shrinking to Expanding (Without Apology)

Shrinking is learned long before it is named.
It is the silent agreement to move carefully,
to speak softly,
to exist in ways that do not unsettle or disrupt.

Shrinking promises safety.
It promises acceptance in exchange for invisibility.
It promises belonging, but only if the self remains manageable.

But shrinking, no matter how skillful,
never delivers the life it promises.
It delivers a life where approval is confused with connection,
where being tolerated is mistaken for being loved.

Expansion asks for more.
It asks for the courage to take up the space once surrendered.
It asks for the willingness to move without apology,
to speak without self-correction,
to exist without constant translation.

Expansion is not about arrogance.
It is not about becoming larger than others.
It is about becoming fully oneself,
without trimming the edges for the comfort of the room.

To expand is to say, with presence not volume:
I am allowed to be all of me here.

No apologies for the emotions that run deep.
No shrinking from the instincts that feel loud.
No disguising the hunger for a life that feels wide enough to hold the whole self.

Expansion is not a threat to others.
It is an invitation—
to meet in the space where neither has to shrink to stay close.

The shift from shrinking to expanding is not a one-time act.
It is a practice:
to notice when the old reflex to disappear arises,
to stay present when the instinct is to retreat,
to trust that the life meant to be lived requires the full size of the self, not the edited version.

And it begins quietly:
with one deep breath taken without apology.
One step forward without retreat.
One truth spoken without shrinking from its echo.

Your Right to Be Loud, Soft, Uncertain, and Here

Taking up space is not about being loud all the time.
It is not about certainty masquerading as strength.
It is not about claiming presence through force.

It is about something quieter, more radical:
the right to be however you are—
loud or soft,
certain or uncertain,
clear or searching—
and to remain present in that truth without apology.

Some days the voice will rise.
Other days it will falter.
Some days the heart will know exactly what it wants.
Other days it will wander through the unknown, fumbling for
clarity.

None of this disqualifies presence.
None of this negates the right to stay.

The world often rewards certainty, performance, bravado.
But real presence is not conditional.
It does not require constant assurance.
It does not require shrinking on the days when confidence runs
thin.

Presence is a practice of staying with oneself,
even when the self feels unfinished,

even when the self feels raw,
even when the self feels uncertain.

The right to take up space is not reserved for the days when
everything feels steady.
It is a right that holds steady through every fluctuation—
through every trembling voice,
every unsure step,
every moment when just being here feels like the bravest act of
all.

You are allowed to be loud without being dismissed as too much.
You are allowed to be soft without being mistaken for weak.
You are allowed to be uncertain without being seen as lost.
You are allowed to be here—fully, imperfectly, honestly.

Not because of what you produce,
or how well you perform,
but simply because you exist.

Practices of Radical Occupation

Radical occupation is not loud by necessity.
It is not a grand gesture,
not a declaration shouted into the world.

It is daily, deliberate, often unseen.

It is choosing to stay in the body when the instinct is to
disappear.
It is choosing to speak when silence feels safer.
It is choosing to breathe fully, stand fully, exist fully—
not just in moments of certainty, but precisely in moments of
doubt.

Radical occupation looks like small acts of self-loyalty:
Holding eye contact a moment longer than feels comfortable.
Walking into a room without adjusting posture to appear smaller.
Taking up physical space without apology—crossed legs
uncrossed, shoulders relaxed, spine tall.

It looks like emotional presence:
Allowing anger to be felt without filtering.
Allowing joy to be expressed without minimizing.
Allowing sorrow to surface without shame.

It looks like conversational honesty:
Saying no when no is true.
Saying yes only when yes is true.
Speaking without diluting, explaining, or shrinking the fullness of
what needs to be said.

Radical occupation is not about dominance.
It is about dignity.
It is about choosing not to vacate the self for the sake of comfort
—

yours or anyone else's.

It is about trusting that being fully here,
even when messy, uncertain, vulnerable,
is a form of truth-telling the world needs more of.

The practices are not heroic.
They are human.
They are the everyday acts by which the self slowly, steadily,
unapologetically reclaims its right to exist without shrinking.

Radical occupation is not something earned.
It is something remembered.
A quiet vow:
I will not leave myself behind.
Not for approval.
Not for ease.
Not for anything.

Love That Doesn't Ask You to Shrink

The New Standard: Love That Honors Expansion

For too long, love has been confused with tolerance.
With endurance.
With the quiet, persistent shrinking of self to fit into spaces too small to hold the truth of who someone really is.

But real love—love worth staying for—does not ask for shrinking.
It does not demand that desires be made smaller,
that emotions be more manageable,
that dreams be trimmed to fit within someone else's comfort.

The new standard for love must be higher.
It must be love that honors expansion.
Love that makes room for growth even when it's inconvenient,
even when it challenges the old, familiar ways of being.

Love that honors expansion does not fear change.
It does not punish transformation.
It recognizes that aliveness is dynamic,
and that loving someone means loving not just who they have been,
but who they are becoming.

This kind of love is not without challenge.
It requires courage—
the courage to stay present through the discomfort of growth,

to witness transformation without demanding its halt,
to celebrate the ways another's light shifts, brightens, and
sometimes blinds.

The new standard is not love that fits into old patterns.
It is love that breaks patterns open.

It is not love that asks for less.
It is love that invites more:
more truth,
more depth,
more presence.

This is the standard:
Love that does not require shrinking as a condition for staying
close.
Love that leaves room for the whole self to breathe, stretch, and
become.

Spotting Love Bombs vs. Love Roots

Not all love is built to last.
Some love arrives in a rush—
overwhelming, consuming, urgent.

It flatters the senses.
It floods the body with attention and affirmation.
It promises everything quickly: belonging, safety, permanence.

But love that arrives as a bomb is unstable.
It detonates with intensity, but it cannot sustain itself.
It demands more than it can hold.
It exhausts rather than nourishes.

Love bombs ask for loyalty without offering roots.
They ask for quick surrender without building real trust.
They create closeness through speed, not depth.
And too often, they require shrinking—
shrinking of needs,
shrinking of instincts,
shrinking of doubts—
to maintain the illusion of immediate perfection.

Love roots grow differently.

Roots take time.
They require patience.
They require staying when the newness wears off.
They require tending when discomfort surfaces.
They require honoring growth, even when it's inconvenient.

Roots don't demand shrinking.
They make room.

Love rooted in patience, trust, and depth doesn't rush the
process.
It doesn't fear change.
It doesn't punish uncertainty.

It allows for expansion because it knows that real connection is
not threatened by growth.
It is strengthened by it.

Spotting the difference is essential:
Love bombs dazzle but demand diminishment.
Love roots endure because they allow for the full unfolding of the
self.

Real love doesn't explode.
It deepens.
It weathers.
It grows.

Intimacy with Someone Who Doesn't Flinch at Depth

Depth tests love.
Not in grand, dramatic moments—
but in the slow, steady unveiling of what is real.

Depth reveals the contradictions.
The unresolved grief.
The unhealed wounds.
The needs too complex to be met with simple answers.

Intimacy with someone who doesn't flinch at depth is rare.
It requires more than affection.
It requires more than compatibility.
It requires a willingness to sit in what is uncomfortable,
to stay present with what is unresolved,
to witness without rushing to fix or flee.

Many are drawn to the surface—the ease of familiarity, the
lightness of beginnings.
But depth asks for more.
It asks for a steadiness not easily found.
A tolerance for nuance.
A patience for imperfection.
A reverence for what can't be easily explained or quickly solved.

To be met in depth is to be seen not as a project,
but as a person.
Not as someone to rescue,
but as someone to respect.

It is to be known in the spaces where vulnerability feels most dangerous,
and to find that connection does not collapse there—
it strengthens.

Someone who doesn't flinch at depth will not ask for shrinking.
They will not retreat when emotions become unwieldy.
They will not shame the hungers that linger just beneath the surface.

They will stay.
They will listen.
They will honor the weight and width of what it means to be fully human.

Intimacy at this level is not about perfection.
It is about presence.

The quiet, steady presence of someone who knows that true closeness begins
where the performance ends.

You Don't Have to Explain Yourself to Be Loved

Love, when it is real, does not demand constant explanation.
It does not require footnotes for feelings,
apologies for needs,
justifications for being exactly as you are.

Love that requires shrinking asks for performance.
Love that honors expansion asks for presence—
presence without performance,
connection without condition.

You don't have to explain why you feel deeply.
Why you need what you need.
Why your heart pulls toward what it pulls toward.

You don't have to defend your softness,
or rationalize your boundaries,
or tone yourself down to stay lovable.

Love that is real sees complexity and does not ask it to be
simplified.
It sees contradiction and does not ask it to be resolved.
It sees growth and does not fear what cannot be controlled.

You don't have to explain your scars,
your dreams,
your silence,
your hunger.

You don't have to be less complicated to be worthy of staying.

The love that asks for constant explanation is not love—
it is management.

Real love does not require a continuous translation of your being.
It holds space for what is still unfinished.
It trusts what is still unfolding.

You are not a riddle to solve.
You are not a project to fix.
You are not a puzzle that needs to be made easier to
understand.

You are a life to be witnessed,
a heart to be honored,
a presence to be met without demand.

And the love that finds you there,
without asking you to explain yourself,
is the love that will not ask you to shrink to stay.

Showing Up Unapologetically (Even When Shaky)

Courage Is What You Do When the Fear Stays

Courage is often misunderstood.
It is mistaken for fearlessness,
for the absence of doubt,
for the steady hand and unwavering heart.

But courage, in its truest form, is not the absence of fear.
It is the decision to move anyway—
to speak anyway,
to show up anyway,
to stay present even when every instinct calls for retreat.

Fear does not vanish with growth.
It evolves.
It follows new edges,
meets new thresholds,
accompanies every step that moves further into authenticity.

The presence of fear is not a sign that something is wrong.
It is a sign that something matters.
It is a sign that the self is being asked to live more fully,
to risk more honestly,
to stay more present.

Courage is what you do when the fear stays.
It is the choice to take the breath,
to speak the truth,
to cross the threshold even when the ground feels unsteady.

It is not boldness without tremble.
It is trembling, honored.

It is not certainty without question.
It is questioning, carried forward.

Courage does not eliminate fear.
It walks alongside it,
refusing to let it be the only voice in the room.

This is the heart of showing up unapologetically:
not waiting for the fear to leave,
but choosing presence even while carrying it.

Honesty Without Performance

Performance is a quiet reflex.
It creeps in when honesty feels too exposed,
when the risk of being fully seen feels too great.

Performance dresses up truth.
It softens the edges.
It makes vulnerability more palatable,
more likable,
more acceptable.

But performance, even when subtle, creates distance.
It turns honesty into a presentation rather than a presence.
It invites applause rather than real connection.

Honesty without performance is riskier.
It does not offer the safety of pre-approved narratives.
It does not guarantee being understood.
It does not smooth discomfort for the sake of keeping peace.

Honesty without performance is raw,
sometimes messy,
sometimes incomplete.
It does not rush to package experience in a way that will be
easier for others to digest.

It says:
Here is the truth, even if it is complicated.
Here is the story, even if it is unfinished.
Here is the self, even if it is trembling.

Honesty without performance trusts that connection built on realness,
even if harder won,
will be stronger, deeper, more sustaining.

It refuses to barter away authenticity for the fleeting security of being liked.

Showing up without performance is not about oversharing.
It is not about spilling everything unfiltered.

It is about offering what is true without rehearsing,
without curating,
without disguising.

It is about trusting that the right people,
the ones who can meet depth with depth,
do not require a version of the self
smoothed into something smaller than truth.

You Will Not Be for Everyone—That Is Liberation

Showing up fully comes with a cost:
not everyone will stay.

Some will drift away when the self is no longer edited to meet
their expectations.
Some will grow uncomfortable when the version of you they knew
expands beyond their comfort.

Not being for everyone is not a failure.
It is not a flaw to fix.

It is the inevitable result of living honestly.

When the self is fully present—untidy, unpolished, unguarded—
it will not resonate with every room,
every audience,
every relationship.

This truth, once accepted, becomes a kind of freedom.

It frees the self from the exhausting work of contortion.
It frees the heart from the hollow currency of constant approval.
It frees life from the pursuit of being universally palatable.

To be for everyone would require being less.
Less clear.
Less present.
Less whole.

Liberation is found not in being chosen by all,
but in belonging to oneself without condition.

It is found in the clarity that comes when no longer measuring
worth by external acceptance.

It is found in the relationships that remain—
the ones that do not ask for dimming or softening or shrinking.

It is found in the quiet rooms where the self can exist without
explanation,
without defense,
without disguise.

You will not be for everyone.
But you were never meant to be.

You are here to be real,
not to be universally approved.

And in that realness,
there is a different kind of belonging—
a belonging that begins, finally, with the self.

What It Feels Like to Stay Instead of Shape-Shift

Staying is a different kind of work.
Not the work of adapting,
not the work of performing,
not the work of calculating what version of the self will be safest
or most accepted.

Staying is quieter, but heavier.
It asks for presence without pretense.
It asks for stillness without apology.

It feels exposed at first—
as if stepping out from behind a carefully constructed shelter.

Without the old reflex to shape-shift,
there is a rawness,
a sense of standing in the open.

But with time, staying begins to feel different:
less like exposure,
more like anchoring.

It feels like breathing without restraint.
It feels like speaking without rehearsing.
It feels like belonging not because the self has been made more palatable,
but because it has been made visible.

Staying feels uncomfortable—
especially when the old reflexes pull hard,

when silence feels safer than truth,
when dimming feels easier than being seen.

But it also feels liberating.
It feels like being in the room without leaving parts of the self
behind at the door.
It feels like trusting that whoever stays, stays for the realness,
and whoever leaves was never staying for the right reasons
anyway.

To stay instead of shape-shift is to make peace with discomfort.
It is to choose alignment over approval.
It is to live without abandoning the self for the comfort of others.

And in that staying,
something steady grows—
a quiet dignity,
a deep resilience,
a belonging that no performance could ever secure.

Making Peace With Your Own Depth

You Are Not a Problem to Solve

Depth often feels like a burden in a world that rewards surfaces.
It can seem like an inconvenience—too intense, too complex, too
much.

The temptation is to treat depth as something to manage,
something to edit,
something to soften.

It is easy to mistake complexity for a flaw,
to believe that feeling deeply, questioning often,
hungering for more—
is a problem to be solved.

But depth is not a defect.
It is not an error in design.
It is not something to fix, cure, or explain away.

Depth is capacity.
Capacity to sit with contradiction.
Capacity to hold both joy and sorrow without collapsing.
Capacity to stay present in a world that often demands speed
over substance.

You are not a problem to solve.
You are a life to be honored—

a life that holds multitudes,
that asks difficult questions,
that feels what others might only glance at.

The work is not to dilute this depth,
not to streamline it into something easier to carry.
The work is to make peace with it—
to recognize it not as a liability,
but as a kind of wisdom.

Making peace with your own depth is not resignation.
It is reverence.
A decision to stop fighting the parts of the self that were never
wrong to begin with.

You are not here to be simple.
You are not here to be easily explained.
You are not here to be smaller than your full self.

You are not a problem to solve.
You are a depth to be lived.

Sensitivity as Superpower

Sensitivity has long been framed as fragility.
As something to outgrow.
As something to manage, to hide, to apologize for.

But sensitivity is not weakness.
It is a form of intelligence.
A way of reading the world beyond what is immediately visible.
A way of feeling the undercurrents most people miss.

Sensitivity catches what others overlook:
the tension beneath the smile,
the unspoken longing in a quiet room,
the truth hiding just beneath casual words.

It is not a flaw.
It is a capacity—
a capacity for nuance, for empathy, for deep seeing.

The world may try to tell a different story.
It may reward detachment,
praise indifference,
celebrate the ability to move through life untouched.

But what the world calls toughness often comes at the cost of
aliveness.
Sensitivity, though sometimes overwhelming, is a form of staying
awake.
It is the refusal to numb.
It is the insistence on caring even when it hurts.

Sensitivity allows for deeper connection.
It allows for real presence.
It allows for the kind of listening that can hear what isn't said.

To carry sensitivity is to carry a superpower—
not because it protects from pain,
but because it makes a richer life possible.

A life that feels fully,
connects deeply,
loves fiercely.

A life that is not protected from ache,
but is wide enough to hold it without shutting down.

Sensitivity is not something to fix.
It is something to honor.

It is not a liability.
It is a superpower.

Loving the Parts That Still Hurt

There will always be parts that remain tender.
Parts that flinch when touched,
parts that carry the memory of old wounds.

Healing does not mean erasing these parts.
It does not mean sealing every crack,
silencing every ache,
forgetting every scar.

Some parts do not disappear.
They soften.
They live differently in the body—
not as open wounds,
but as quiet reminders of where the self has been broken and
remade.

Loving the parts that still hurt is not indulgence.
It is care.
It is refusing to exile the versions of the self that endured,
the ones that survived without the luxury of healing on schedule.

These parts do not need fixing.
They need tending.

A hand placed gently over the ache,
not to push it away,
but to say:
You are welcome here too.

A patience offered to the parts that do not move as quickly,
that do not trust as easily,
that do not forgive as readily.

Loving the parts that still hurt is choosing not to rush healing.
It is allowing tenderness to have a seat at the table of the self,
not as an embarrassment,
but as a testament.

A testament to endurance.
A testament to care.
A testament to the reality that wholeness does not mean
unbrokenness.

The parts that still hurt are not proof of failure.
They are proof of humanity.

Loving them is not a delay on the road to becoming whole.
It is part of the arrival.

Depth Without Drama, Truth Without Noise

Depth does not require spectacle.
It does not need to announce itself loudly to be real.
It does not seek validation through chaos or noise.

True depth is quiet.
It is the ability to sit with discomfort without turning it into a
performance.
It is the capacity to hold complexity without needing to dramatize
it.

Depth without drama is steady.
It allows emotion to rise and fall without needing an audience.
It honors intensity without turning it into currency.
It chooses presence over performance.

Similarly, truth does not need to shout to be powerful.
It does not need to be sharpened into confrontation to matter.
It does not need noise to make itself known.

Truth, when lived rather than proclaimed, moves differently.
It moves quietly,
settling into the spaces where posturing cannot reach.
It shapes actions rather than arguments.
It builds trust rather than demanding agreement.

Living with depth means resisting the temptation to turn pain into
identity.
It means letting experiences shape without defining.
It means letting wounds inform without leading.

Living with truth means refusing to weaponize honesty.
It means speaking what is real without needing to be louder than everyone else.
It means trusting that truth, lived quietly and steadily, carries its own weight.

Depth without drama.
Truth without noise.

This is how peace is made with the self—
not by shouting to be seen,
but by standing steady in what is already known.

A kind of quietness that is not absence,
but presence.

A kind of strength that is not force,
but foundation.

The Art of Not Abandoning Yourself

The Subtle Ways We Leave Ourselves Behind

Self-abandonment rarely announces itself.
It is not always a grand betrayal or a dramatic departure.
It is quieter, more ordinary.
It happens in the small choices made without noticing:
the silence instead of the truth,
the smile instead of the boundary,
the nod instead of the no.

It is in the moments when instinct says stay, but habit says leave.
When the heart tightens, and the response is to override it.
When discomfort rises, and the reflex is to minimize it for the
sake of peace.

Self-abandonment looks like agreement when disagreement
trembles in the throat.
It looks like enduring when departure would be more honest.
It looks like disappearing from the self to be visible to others.

These moments are easy to miss because they are woven into
the fabric of daily living.
Conditioned by years of learning that being liked is safer than
being whole.
That being easy is safer than being real.

But each small departure adds up.
Each moment of leaving the self behind leaves a trace—
a sense of disconnection that deepens over time,
a weariness that no amount of external approval can fully erase.

Self-abandonment is not just about relationships with others.
It is about the relationship with the self—
the quiet agreements made, moment by moment,
either to stay present or to disappear.

Not abandoning yourself does not begin with grand declarations.
It begins with noticing:
noticing the instinct to shrink,
the impulse to smooth over,
the moment the self steps aside for the sake of comfort.

And in that noticing,
the possibility of staying grows.

Choosing Yourself in Real Time

Choosing yourself is not a one-time vow.
It is not a dramatic stand taken once and held forever.
It is a practice—
a choice made again and again,
moment by moment,
in the quiet spaces where no one else is watching.

It happens in real time,
in the milliseconds between instinct and action,
in the pause where the old reflex to abandon can be interrupted.

Choosing yourself looks like speaking up when silence feels
safer.
It looks like stepping back when staying would mean shrinking.
It looks like saying yes only when yes is true,
and no even when no is inconvenient.

Choosing yourself does not always feel good in the moment.
It can feel disruptive.
It can feel selfish to a mind trained for self-erasure.
It can feel dangerous to a heart conditioned to survive through
compliance.

But real-time loyalty to the self is where wholeness is built—
not in theory,
not in aspiration,
but in practice.

Choosing yourself means trusting the small, subtle signals:
the tightening in the gut,
the quickening of the heart,
the whisper that says:
This matters.
This is not okay.
This is who I am.

Choosing yourself is not an abandonment of others.
It is an end to abandoning the self in order to keep others
comfortable.

It is a return, again and again,
to the quiet knowing that wholeness cannot be outsourced,
that dignity cannot be negotiated,
that truth cannot be sacrificed without cost.

Choosing yourself is an act of presence,
an act of courage,
an act of remembering who you are—
especially when it would be easier to forget.

Staying Present Through Discomfort

Discomfort is not a signal that something has gone wrong.
It is often a sign that something true is surfacing.
A boundary being honored.
A pattern being broken.
A self being reclaimed.

Staying present through discomfort is one of the hardest parts of
not abandoning yourself.
It asks for more than noticing.
It asks for staying—
for resisting the pull to retreat, to soften, to explain away.

Discomfort will arrive like a tide:
the racing heart,
the tightened throat,
the silence that feels unbearable.

It will tempt with old exits:
the easy agreement,
the polite smile,
the familiar vanishing act.

But staying—truly staying—means breathing into the tension
without folding.
It means sitting with the ache of being misunderstood.
It means feeling the weight of unmet expectations without
collapsing under it.

Staying present through discomfort is not about tolerating harm.
It is about recognizing that discomfort is different from danger.
It is about learning to tell the difference between the two.

Discomfort is the body learning to trust itself again.
It is the heart learning to stand its ground.
It is the mind learning that being seen is survivable,
even when it feels unbearably raw.

Each moment of staying builds something unseen but vital:
resilience without hardness,
clarity without defensiveness,
presence without apology.

To stay present through discomfort is not to reject ease,
but to build a life where ease is real because it is earned through
truth,
not borrowed through pretense.

It is to live in a way that is not painless,
but honest.
Not effortless,
but free.

Self-Loyalty as a Daily Practice

Self-loyalty is not a grand act.
It is not a one-time decision carved in stone.
It is a daily practice,
built in the smallest of moments.

It is a series of quiet choices:
to honor what is true instead of what is easy,
to stay present instead of disappearing,
to protect the self without apology.

Self-loyalty is not rigid.
It is not about refusing to change or grow.
It is about changing in the direction of truth,
growing in ways that do not require abandonment of what
matters most.

It is not loud.
It does not need constant affirmation.
It builds silently, like a muscle strengthened through repeated
use—
moment by moment,
boundary by boundary,
truth by truth.

Self-loyalty asks:
What does it mean to stay with myself today?
What would it look like to honor what I know, even if it costs
comfort?
What would it feel like to belong first and always to myself?

The practice is not perfect.
There will be moments of hesitation,
moments of faltering,
moments of forgetting.

But self-loyalty does not demand perfection.
It asks only for return.
A returning to the self after every small departure.
A choosing again and again not to leave.

Over time, self-loyalty becomes less an effort,
and more a way of being—
a quiet steadiness,
a groundedness that no approval or rejection can shake.

It becomes the foundation for a life that does not require
performance,
a love that does not require shrinking,
a presence that does not require explanation.

Self-loyalty is not an act of selfishness.
It is an act of reverence—
for the life,
the heart,
the wholeness
that were never meant to be bartered away.

From Fixing to Witnessing

People Don't Need Your Fix—They Need Your Fullness

It is tempting to believe that love means fixing.
That care is best expressed through solutions,
that presence must be earned through action.

But most people do not need to be fixed.
They do not need quick answers,
or patched wounds,
or neatly packaged advice.

They need presence.
They need fullness.
They need someone willing to stay without rushing to improve
what is complicated.

Fixing creates distance.
It positions one person as whole and the other as broken.
It turns relationship into transaction—
I will stay if I can make this better.

Witnessing is different.
Witnessing says:
I will stay even if I can't make this better.
I will stay because being here matters more than having the right
words.

151

I will stay without needing to rescue you from your own experience.

Fullness is not about perfection.
It is about showing up whole—
as a person who carries their own unresolved questions,
who does not need to solve to stay close.

Fullness says:
I trust your process.
I trust your capacity to carry your own life.
I trust that being with you, not fixing you, is what matters most.

People don't need your solutions.
They need your presence.
They need your willingness to be with what is raw and real and unresolved.

They need not your fixing,
but your fullness.

How to Hold Space Without Disappearing Into It

Holding space is often misunderstood.
It is not about absorbing the pain of others.
It is not about becoming weightless,
invisible,
selfless to the point of disappearance.

Real holding is not self-erasure.
It does not require shrinking to make room.
It does not require silence at the cost of selfhood.
It does not ask the witness to vanish to validate the one being
seen.

To hold space well,
you have to remain fully present—
not as a shadow,
but as a steady self.

Holding space means staying grounded in your own being
while offering presence to another's.
It is the act of listening without losing yourself.
Of caring without collapsing.

It is knowing where you end and the other begins.
It is knowing that empathy does not mean enmeshment.
That support does not require self-abandonment.

The one who holds space is not empty.
They are rooted.
They are steady enough to allow another's experience without

rushing to fix it,
to carry it,
to control it.

Holding space without disappearing requires boundaries—
the quiet, firm kind that honor both selves:
the one speaking,
and the one listening.

It is an offering that says:
I will be with you without becoming you.
I will witness without disappearing.

True presence is not weightless.
It has form,
substance,
integrity.

It is not about vanishing into the other's pain.
It is about standing near it,
steady and whole,
trusting that presence,
not rescue,
is the most powerful gift you can give.

Being With vs. Doing For

It is easy to confuse presence with intervention.
To believe that to love someone is to do for them what they
cannot yet do for themselves.

But being with is different from doing for.

Doing for says:
I don't trust you to carry this.
Let me take it from you.
Let me solve it so you don't have to suffer.

Doing for can seem compassionate on the surface.
But underneath, it often carries the belief that struggle is a failure,
that discomfort must be rescued,
that difficulty must be erased for love to be real.

Being with says something different.
It says:
I trust you to navigate your own life.
I will not rescue you from what is yours to carry.
I will stay present without trying to change or fix what you are
living.

Being with is the harder work.
It asks for patience.
It asks for humility—
the humility to know that love is not control,
that presence is enough.

It asks for the ability to stay close without taking over,
to care deeply without assuming responsibility for outcomes.

Being with respects sovereignty.
It respects the other's process,
their timing,
their pain.

It says:
I see you in this, and I will not leave you alone with it.
But I will also not step in front of you.
I will not take your life out of your hands.

Being with trusts that bearing witness is not passive.
It is active in its patience,
radical in its respect,
powerful in its refusal to fix what must be lived through.

Learning to Witness Yourself

Witnessing is not only something offered to others.
It is a practice that must also be turned inward.

Learning to witness yourself means learning to stay present with
your own life,
without rushing to fix it,
to judge it,
to rewrite it into something neater than it really is.

It means sitting with your own contradictions,
your own unfinished stories,
your own complicated truths,
without demanding that they resolve on a schedule.

It means offering to the self the same patience so often extended
to others:
the patience to let hurt unfold without silencing it,
the patience to let joy surface without minimizing it,
the patience to let becoming be as slow and messy as it needs to
be.

Witnessing yourself is not passive.
It is active attention.
It is choosing to stay close to your own experience without
abandoning it when it becomes inconvenient or uncomfortable.

It is refusing to fracture yourself into acceptable and
unacceptable pieces.
It is refusing to abandon the parts still tender,

still uncertain,
still in progress.

Witnessing yourself is an act of loyalty.
It is the decision to remain present in your own life,
even when the instinct is to escape it.

It is the practice of offering the self the same reverence you have
long offered to others:
a willingness to be with what is real without rushing to make it
prettier,
easier,
more acceptable.

To witness yourself is to live without constant repair.
It is to trust that being present is enough.
That wholeness is not the absence of flaws,
but the presence of selfhood fully inhabited.

Staying Open When It Would Be Easier to Disappear

The Soft Armor of Receptivity

Openness is not weakness.
It is not naivety,
not blind trust,
not an invitation for harm.

Openness is an armor of a different kind—
not the rigid, brittle shield of defense,
but the soft, resilient armor of receptivity.

Receptivity is not about letting everything in.
It is about remaining porous enough to be touched by life,
without being dismantled by it.

It is about feeling fully without collapsing.
Caring deeply without losing shape.
Trusting selectively without shutting down completely.

Receptivity is a form of strength that does not announce itself.
It allows for tenderness without surrendering sovereignty.
It allows for hope without forfeiting discernment.
It allows for love without erasing boundaries.

In a world that rewards hardness,
receptivity is rebellion.

It is a refusal to become impermeable.
A refusal to let disappointment harden the heart into a fortress.
A refusal to disappear behind cynicism and detachment.

The soft armor of receptivity is not passivity.
It is engagement—
with caution when needed,
with courage when called for,
with care always.

Staying open is not the absence of fear.
It is moving forward with fear held gently,
not as a master,
but as a companion.

This is what allows staying open when it would be easier to
disappear:
the quiet decision to wear the soft armor of presence,
to meet the world without vanishing from it.

Choosing Openness Without Losing Safety

Openness does not mean surrendering safety.
It does not mean exposing everything without discernment,
or trusting everyone without boundary.

True openness is intentional.
It is selective.
It is the deliberate act of allowing in what aligns with truth
while keeping what is harmful at a distance.

Safety and openness are not opposites.
They are companions.
They shape each other, balance each other, strengthen each
other.

Safety makes openness sustainable.
It offers a container—
a sense of groundedness that allows for risk without
recklessness,
for vulnerability without collapse.

Choosing openness without losing safety is about knowing:
when to step forward and when to hold back,
when to reveal and when to remain still,
when to trust the body's signals that say:
This is not for me.
This is not safe.

It is not about being unguarded.
It is about being self-guarded,

161

self-trusting,
self-honoring.

It is openness that flows from sovereignty,
not from longing to be seen at any cost.

It is the kind of openness that knows:
boundaries do not block love;
they make real love possible.

Choosing openness without losing safety is the art of staying
reachable
without being overrun.
Of staying visible
without being violated.

It is the quiet skill of carrying both tenderness and discernment,
allowing the heart to remain open
without offering it to hands that cannot hold it.

Letting Love In Without Performing for It

Real love cannot be earned through performance.
It does not arrive as a reward for being pleasing enough,
careful enough,
perfect enough.

Yet it is easy to slip into old patterns—
to perform in the hope of being chosen,
to curate the self into something more digestible,
more lovable.

Performance may invite approval,
but it cannot sustain real connection.
It trades authenticity for applause,
but applause is not the same as love.

Letting love in without performing for it asks for something
harder:
to stand as you are,
to stay as you are,
to receive as you are—
without softening truths or sharpening edges to fit someone
else's comfort.

It asks for the courage to believe that love can find you in your
fullness,
not just in your presentation.
That love can hold you without needing you to be smaller,
safer,
less.

Letting love in without performance requires trust—
trust in the self that stays whole,
even when love feels uncertain.
Trust in the kind of love that deepens, not because you
performed well enough,
but because you remained real enough.

It means staying rooted in your own life,
your own body,
your own truth—
allowing love to meet you there,
rather than chasing it into places where you no longer recognize
yourself.

Love that requires performance is not love.
It is transaction.

Real love arrives when there is no act to maintain,
no role to rehearse,
no mask to hold in place.

Letting love in without performing for it is not passive.
It is active surrender.
It is radical honesty.
It is receiving, not earning.

It is the quiet, powerful refusal to disappear in order to be held.

Living as If Nothing About You Needs to Be Dimmed

To live without dimming is not an act of arrogance.
It is an act of alignment—
a commitment to carry your own light
without shrinking it for rooms that prefer shadows.

Dimming happens slowly.
In the polite silences.
In the measured tones.
In the careful edits made to soften the truth of who you are.

But living fully—
living as if nothing about you needs to be dimmed—
requires a different posture.
It requires standing without apology.
Speaking without dilution.
Existing without asking for permission.

It does not mean being unkind.
It does not mean being inflexible.
It means trusting that who you are, in your depth and complexity,
in your tenderness and ferocity,
does not require reduction to be worthy of space.

It means believing that your voice does not need to be softened
to be heard.
That your feelings do not need to be minimized to be valid.
That your dreams do not need to be shrunk to be acceptable.

Living as if nothing about you needs to be dimmed is radical
because it is rare.
Rare to see someone occupy their life fully,
without bending themselves to fit the expectations of others.

It is not about being louder.
It is about being truer.

It is not about being invulnerable.
It is about being visible,
even when visibility feels dangerous.

To live this way is to carry a different kind of steadiness—
a steadiness that does not demand understanding from
everyone,
only integrity with yourself.

It is to say:
I will not trade belonging to myself for acceptance from others.
I will not edit myself down to the parts that are easiest to love.
I will stay whole, even when wholeness costs comfort.

This is how staying open becomes living fully—
not by eliminating risk,
but by refusing to disappear.

Not by becoming invincible,
but by becoming undimmed.

Manifesto: You Are Not Too Much

You are not too sensitive.
You are not too emotional.
You are not too intense.
You are not too complicated.
You are not too much.

You are the exact amount of life this world needs.

You were not made to be small.
You were not made to be silent.
You were not made to dim so others could shine more
comfortably.

Your depth is not a flaw to be managed.
Your feelings are not excess to be trimmed.
Your hunger for truth, for connection, for wholeness—
is not too much to ask of the world.

You were made to take up space.
To love without shrinking.
To speak without softening.
To feel without apology.
To stay without shape-shifting.

You are allowed to live without explanation.
You are allowed to need without justification.
You are allowed to want what feels like too much for rooms that
were never built to hold you.

You are allowed to remain whole,
even when the cost is discomfort.

Even when the reward is solitude.
Even when the world calls your fullness a problem to solve.

You are not too much.
You are not wrong for being whole.

This life—your life—was never meant to be bargained down.
It was meant to be lived undimmed.
It was meant to be carried in its fullness.
It was meant to be witnessed in its depth.
It was meant to be stayed with—by you most of all.

Do not quiet yourself to be digestible.
Do not fold yourself to fit a space you were made to outgrow.
Do not disappear to be loved.

You are not too much.
You are exactly enough.

About the Author

Ethan Starke writes for those who have been told they are too much—too sensitive, too emotional, too alive for a world that often rewards detachment over depth.

A lifelong student of emotional truth and human connection, Ethan Starke is known for work that refuses quick fixes in favor of the slow, steady excavation of authenticity. With a voice that blends psychological insight, spiritual clarity, and lived experience, Ethan invites readers to return to the parts of themselves the world asked them to abandon.

Their books are not instruction manuals. They are invitations— into deeper self-loyalty, into unapologetic wholeness, into living undimmed.

Ethan Starke is the author of:

- *You Are Not Too Much*
- *The Science of Letting Go*
- *The Fire That Consumes Nothing*
- *You Can't Optimize This*
- *Curate a Date* (for those seeking to deepen connection without performance)

Through words rooted in lived experience, Ethan Starke offers what so many crave: not more ways to improve, but real ways to come home to themselves.